who knew?

Odor
Eliminating
Miracles

Hints and
Tips for the
Freshest Home

Cover design by Michele L. Trombley

ISBN: 978-0-9883264-1-5

Printed and bound in the United States of America

2 4 6 8 10 9 7 5 4 3 1

Please visit us online at www.WhoKnewTips.com

TABLE OF CONTENTS

Introduction

Who knew there were so many different odors in your home? And so many different ways to get rid of them all? Whether it's a smelly shower, a stinky microwave, or musty clothing, this book is full of tips to expel unwanted odors from your home. Plus, you'll save tons of money with our chapter on DIY air fresheners that are easy and fun to make.

The first part of this book concentrates on tips for specific areas of your home to clean and make odor-free. The second part is chock full of information about making your own air fresheners, eliminating pet odors, and keeping your car and yard sparkling and smelling fresh. There's even a bonus chapter on how to rid bugs from your home. And don't forget to visit us at WhoKnewTips.com for even more ways to save!

Thriftily yours,
Jeanne and Bruce

CHAPTER 1

Freshening Up Around Your Home

Unwanted Perfume

Someone gave you perfume as a present and although it smells nice, it's just not your cup of tea. Instead of spraying it on yourself, use it to freshen rooms in your home. Squirt a small amount near light bulbs, and when you turn on the lights you'll also turn on a lovely scent. You can also use perfume as a refill for a bottle that contains aromatherapy sticks.

Odor Eliminator

Here's an easy spray that will completely neutralize household odors for mere pennies. Fill a 2-cup spray bottle with water and add 2 tablespoons baking soda. Shake before spritzing. You can also add your favorite essential oil for a fresh scent!

Surprising Brass Cleaner

Shine doorknobs, candlesticks, or anything else brass with Worcestershire sauce! Use a few drops on a damp cloth to rub brass clean. You won't believe how shiny it gets until you try it!

Crystal Clean Windows

The best way we've ever found to clean windows? Wet a clean, brown paper bag with vinegar, then wipe away for a streak-free shine.

Be Your Own Mr. Clean

Do you love Mr. Clean Magic Erasers? These costly wonders are made from a material called melamine foam. Melamine foam has been used for decades as an insulator and sound-proofer, which means you can buy large sheets of it for less than the cost of a single box of "magic sponges." Buy some online or at a hardware store, then cut them down to size! They'll cost you less than 30¢ each.

Clean those Keys

Cheese puffs at midnight plus a "Hits of the 80s" YouTube marathon was one of your classic "seemed like a good idea at the time" ideas. Don't worry; the next morning you can clean the computer keyboard with an old toothbrush. Detach from the computer or else make sure the machine is off before you go to work.

Easy Ceiling Fan Clean

Some may say that opening an umbrella in the house is bad luck, but you won't mind the risk when you see how much easier it makes cleaning your ceiling fan. Just hook the handle of an upside-down, open umbrella over the top of the fan, then let the dust that you wipe off the blades fall inside. Close it up when you're done and carefully take outside to dump the dust out.

Lampshade Duster

If you have a pleated lampshade, you know how hard it can be to clean the dust out of those crevices. Our secret weapon? An old paintbrush. It's the perfect size for its soft bristles to get between each crease.

Bottoms Up

Yet another reason we've kept baby wipes around long after our youngest finished nursery school: They work great to soak up carpet stains! Grape juice, red wine, fruit punch? Bring 'em on.

Ceiling Clean

It seems cruel that, after spending so much of your time cleaning your home, dust still manages to get places you never thought to clean—like your ceiling. To vanquish this last bit of dirt, use a clean, dry paint roller with a long arm to dust quickly above your head.

OUR FIVE FAVORITE
Ways to Easily Dust Blinds

1. Is there any chore more annoying than dusting your Venetian blinds? Luckily, you don't have to buy one of those "blinds cleaners." Instead, use bread crusts. Just hold a piece of crust around each slat, then run it along the length of the blinds. An old paintbrush will also do the trick, or you can use the brush attachment on your vacuum cleaner.

2. An easy way to clean blinds is to wrap a kitchen spatula in an old cloth and secure it with a rubber band, then dip it in rubbing alcohol or your favorite cleaner, close the blinds, and go to it!

3. Aluminum blinds are great for keeping out light, but they can be hard to clean! The easiest way to clean smudges off aluminum blinds is with a pencil eraser. Dust will come off with a few swipes of a fabric softener sheet.

4. Give mini blinds a good clean by simply throwing them in the bathtub filled with water and white vinegar or your favorite cleanser. Shake them out well and hang them up wet. There may be a few streaks once they've air-dried, but they're nearly impossible to spot.

5. Stubborn smudges and stains on your window blinds? Lay the shades on a table or countertop and rub the spots with an art-gum eraser (which can be found at art or office supply stores). It will erase the smudges away!

Minimize Broom-Swept Dust

To eliminate the trail of dust your broom leaves behind, fill a spray bottle with three parts water and one part liquid fabric softener, and spray the broom before sweeping. The spritz makes the broom strands more pliable and helps it collect dirt more efficiently.

Paint Odor Remover

To get rid of that overwhelming paint odor after you've redone a room, place a bowl or two of onion slices in the room. They will absorb the smell of the paint.

For Fresh-Smelling Luggage

When you return home from your summer vacation, throw a few dryer sheets in your suitcases before you put them away. The sheets will prevent any musty odors from festering while the bags are stored.

Vanilla Value

Fight odors in smelly places throughout the house (closets, coolers, drawers, etc.) with this nifty trick. Place a damp paper towel in a cup and add a couple teaspoons of vanilla extract. Let it sit for a few days in the stinky spot, and the odor will vanish.

Fresher Flowers

Ever experienced that "unfresh" smell when taking your flowers out of the vase? To keep your cut flowers smelling fresh and lasting longer, make sure you remove any of the stem leaves that will be underwater in your vase. If left underwater, leaves rot quickly. A drop or two of bleach can keep flowers alive for longer. This always struck us as odd, until we stopped to think that you use bleach to kill bacteria, viruses, and "germs" in general. Why not flower germs? You can also add aspirin and a little sugar; or even vodka (yes, vodka!). These ingredients will keep your flowers disease-free.

Not-So-Friendly Fruit

When deciding where to place that beautiful bouquet you just brought home, steer clear of the fruit bowl. Ethylene gas given off by fruit will cause the flowers to die more quickly. Choose a spot far away from any fruit, and your flowers will last longer.

Loosening Soot

If you throw some salt in your fireplace every now and then, soot will be easier to clean from your chimney. It will also make your fire burn a cool yellow color!

Swiffer Savings

Just because you have a wet/dry mop like Swiffer doesn't mean you have to spend a cent on those pricey replacement cloths! Instead, use a sock from your "missing mates" pile and stretch it around the head of the mop. It will work just as well, and you can throw it in the washing machine when you're done!

Super Sweeping

Super-power your broom by covering its bristles with pantyhose. Cut an old pair off at the knee and stretch the toe over the bottom of the broom, then pull up over the bristles and tie at the top. The pulled-taut mesh will catch even the finest dust and dirt, keeping big dust bunnies from gathering in the bristles of your broom.

Groom Your Broom

If your broom has lost its shape, gather the bristles with a rubber band and leave it on for few a days for it to return to its original form. Remove and sweep away. (If that's what you were planning on doing—otherwise just shove it back where it was in the pantry behind the paper towel rack.)

Freshen That Air

Here's an easy way to make your own eco-friendly air freshener with ingredients you have around the house. Mix 2 cups warm water with 2 tablespoons baking soda and ½ teaspoon orange or vanilla extract. It's safe to spray around pets, kids, and most furniture (although you might want to spot-check first).

Good Gravy!

Did your clumsy uncle spill gravy all over your best tablecloth? Not to worry! Just blot up what you can with a paper towel, then sprinkle artificial sweetener or flour over what remains on the tablecloth. After dinner, soak the tablecloth in the washer with your regular detergent for half an hour, then wash as usual.

Battle Dust Bunnies

The easiest way to vacuum under a dresser? Just remove the bottom drawer, and you'll be able to suck up those dust bunnies with ease.

Clean Sweep

If your house is anything like ours, it's rare that the space under the bed is cleared out enough to allow for cleaning. But on those singular occasions when you catch a glimpse of the hardwood floor that first attracted you to the house, don't sweep under the bed—it will only stir the dust up into your box spring. Use a dryer sheet instead. The dust, mites, and other microscopic but pernicious stuff lurking around down there will cling to the sheet and then can simply be thrown away. You can still use a mop or broom to push the sheet around into hard-to-reach places.

Clean Candles Easily

If you have some beautiful candles that have begun to get dusty, cleaning them is easy. Just ball up some old pantyhose and rub them down. Its microfiber is perfect for picking up the dirt without harming your candle.

Lemon Peels for Kindling

The best thing to use as kindling in your fireplace isn't newspaper (or printed out emails from your ex). It's lemon peels! Lemon (and orange) peels smell delicious when they burn, and they contain oils that not only make them burn longer, but help ignite the wood around them. Finally, they produce less creosote than paper, which will help keep your chimney clean.

Stick to Your Gum

Gum may have staying power in your stomach, but not on your sofa. With a little bit of duct tape you can remove a wad stuck on your couch. Wrap a piece of tape around your palm sticky side out and keep dabbing and pulling until you've removed the sticky intruder. You don't even have to interrupt your TV show to complete the task!

Clean Electronics

If your MP3 player has seen better days, give it a quick clean. Our favorite method? A bit of rubbing alcohol or astringent on a clean make-up sponge. Just rub it over the player and it will look as good as new!

Booze It Off

If you're having trouble removing a pesky label, just soak the spot in rubbing alcohol. Leave on for up to a minute, then wipe right off. Don't have any rubbing alcohol? The kind of alcohol you drink—like vodka, rum, or gin—works well, too.

Lemon Aid

Save money on wood cleaners by making your own at home. It's simple: Just combine the juice from one lemon with 2 cups vegetable or olive oil. Use it just like you would a store-bought cleaner!

Smelly Suitcases

Is your suitcase a bit musty? The night before packing, pour a cup of baking soda in it, close it, and shake. In the morning, vacuum up the baking soda and the smell should be gone.

Rejuvenate a Cedar Chest

Cedar chests are wonderful because they not only look great, but their scent keeps moths away, too. But what to do when they begin to lose their scent? Get out some fine sandpaper and go to work! Gently sanding the inside of the chest will bring its scent back to life, making sure your clothes are safe and your room smells wonderful.

Freshen Up Stinky Diapers

If you get a nasty whiff every time you open the diaper pail, drop a few charcoal briquettes under the pail's liner. You'll be amazed at what you don't smell.

Bed Pillow Know-How

Here's an easy way to start your spring-cleaning: Begin with your bed pillows. To make them fluffy and fresh, just place them in the clothes dryer with fabric softener and two clean tennis balls for a few minutes.

Flat Cushion Fix

The beautiful cushions on your chairs are so flattened they're not much more than decoration at this point—now what? Let them sit in the sun for several hours (flipping halfway through) and they'll fluff back up! The sun's warmth is just enough heat to evaporate cushion-flattening moisture, but not enough to damage them (just don't leave them out so long they fade!).

No More Musty Vacuums

Say good-bye to the musty odor emanating from your vacuum with this solution: Put a handful of potpourri into your vacuum bag! Now when you turn your vacuum on, you'll release a lovely scent into the air, making stale smells a thing of the past.

Add Scented Salts for Beautiful Linens

Salt is a miracle worker when it comes to removing linen stains; if you use scented salts in your laundry, you'll get the extra bonus of lovely-smelling sheets. Add ¼ cup scented bath salts during your washing machine's rinse cycle. Not only will your sheets smell great, but the salt acts like a starch to keep them extra crisp. Just make sure not to use bath salts with dyes.

For Sweaty Summers

On sticky summer nights, cool down and freshen up by sprinkling a little baby powder between your sheets before retiring for the night.

Keep Drapes Fresh

Try this nifty trick to make sure your new or recently cleaned drapes stay crisp and fresh: Spray them with a few light coats of unscented hairspray before hanging them up.

For a Great-Smelling Home

When it's too cold to open the windows, freshen your whole house fast by placing a few drops of vanilla extract on your furnace's filter. Your house's heating system will do the rest of the work for you.

Clean Up Sooty Bricks with Cola

Try an old masonry trick to brighten up soot-stained brick. Mix a can of cola with 3½ fluid ounces all-purpose household cleaner and 3½ quarts water in a bucket. Sponge onto sooty brick and leave for 15 minutes. Loosen the soot by scrubbing with a stiff-bristled brush. Sponge with clean water. For a stronger solution, add more cola.

No More Mildew Smell

Does your basement smell like, well, a basement? Try this: Cut an onion in half, and put it on a plate where you smell the mildew. It will smell like an onion for a bit, but afterward, the mildew smell will be gone!

OUR FIVE FAVORITE
Ways to Freshen Up Books

1. If you're placing some old books in storage and don't want them to acquire a musty smell, here's the solution. Place a new sheet of fabric softener inside the pages, and that battered copy of *To Kill a Mockingbird* will stay nice and fresh until you need it again.

2. If you have books that are *already* musty, just place them in a paper grocery bag with an open box of baking soda. Fold over the bag, staple it shut, and let it sit for a week or two. Your books should smell considerably better when you take them out.

3. Make your old, musty book smell like new with this simple trick. Sprinkle ½ inch of cat litter in the bottom of a container that has a lid, then seal the book inside for 12–24 hours. It will come out smelling like a book again.

4. If your books stink, try this tactic for wiping out mildew. Dust mildewed pages with corn flour, French chalk, or talcum powder. Leave it inside the closed book for several days, then brush it off.

5. To help prevent future mildew, place a small container of cat litter or charcoal on the shelf near your books to attract humidity and keep it away from your paperbacks.

Spotless With Salt

For a cleaner, brighter carpet, sprinkle a small amount of salt before you vacuum. The salt provides a mild abrasive cleaning action that won't hurt the fibers.

Deodorize Garbage Cans Naturally

Wash and deodorize trashcans with a solution of 1 teaspoon lemon juice mixed with 1 quart water. Sprinkling baking soda into the bottom of every garbage bag will also help keep odors at bay.

Aromatic Vacuum

To rid your house of pet, cooking, or other smells, add a cotton ball soaked in vanilla or lavender oil to your vacuum cleaner bag. It's a great way to rid your home of an offensive odor by creating a nice scent instead.

Surprising Second Use

It's easy to keep your trashcans from stinking up your home. We like to rip out those perfume strips from magazines and place one at the bottom of every trashcan throughout the house. Or try dryer sheets: They make your clothes smell fresh and wonderful, so they'll work miracles in stinky garbage pails too.

Perk Up a Room

Guests are arriving and you finally enter the guest room that's been closed off for months, only to find that the mattress smells musty even though it's perfectly dry. To solve this problem, turn the mattress and sprinkle a little baking soda on it before you make up the bed with fresh bedding. You can also sprinkle baking soda into pillowcases to freshen up pillows.

Freshen Your Humidifier

Humidifier smelling musty? Add 2 tablespoons lemon juice, and it will never smell fresher!

CHAPTER 2

Neutralizing Odors in the Kitchen and Bathroom

Quick Fix for a Stinky Microwave

Microwave odors? Cut a lemon in quarters and put it in a bowl of water, then place in the microwave on high for 2 minutes. Wipe the inside with a soft cloth and any stains will lift easily.

Spud Scrub

Potatoes come in a nice mesh bag that can be used as a gentle but effective dish scrubber. Remove any staples, scrunch together, and use as you would a scrubby sponge. Wrap two rubber bands around it if you want to keep it from spreading out and taking over the counter in between uses.

Great Grill Cleaner

Your BBQ chicken was a hit, but your grill is a mess. What to do? Poke half an onion, dipped in vegetable oil, on your grill fork, and scrub it over the hot grates. There are enzymes in onions that break down grime, and the oil will help soften the grilled-on gunk.

Wake Up and Smell the Clean Coffee

Cut up stale bread into small pieces and run through your electric coffee grinder to clean the machine naturally. The oil and debris left from the coffee beans will be absorbed into the bread. When you're done, wipe with a rag or paper towel. Bonus points if you can think of a way to use the oily, coffee-flavored breadcrumbs!

Beat Brussels Sprout Smell

Boiling Brussels sprouts can cause a distinct sulfur odor to pervade your kitchen. To prevent this sour smell, just throw a few celery stalks into the pot with the sprouts— they'll absorb the odor and neutralize the scent.

Simple Shelf Cleaner

Vinegar is better than soap when it comes to cleaning the kitchen shelves. Mix a solution of one part vinegar to 10 parts water in a cleaned-out spray bottle. It will naturally disinfect the cabinets without leaving behind a strong smell that can seep into your food.

Tea Party

Here's a terrific way to make your post-dinner clean-up a breeze: Remove cooked-on food from pots and pans effortlessly by filling them with water, adding a tea bag, and simmering. The tea's acid will break up food.

Great for Multitasking

Believe it or not, toothpaste makes a great polish for your faucets. Just rub on and buff off with a soft cloth. The white, non-gel variety works best.

Stove Saver

Here's a tip to impress even your friend who has a superhuman level of household know-how: Use tea to keep gunk from sticking to your stove. Brew a pot of tea that is four times normal strength, then wipe it on your stove. The tannins in the tea will make it hard for grease and food to stick, making cleaning quick and easy.

Simple Solution for a Sparkling Stove

Do the gas burners on your stove need a major make-over? Removing caked-on grime is easy, but it requires calling in the big guns: household ammonia. Pour ¼ cup into a large Ziploc bag, place two burners inside, and seal. Let the fumes work overnight, then rinse and rub with a rag or paper towel. Stovetop perfection!

Blender Cleaner

Wash your blender in less than a minute with this simple trick! Just fill it halfway with hot water, then add a drop of dishwashing liquid, cover with its lid, and hit blend for 30 seconds. Suds will fill your blender and clean it without you having to disassemble the whole contraption.

Vanilla Ice

One of the easiest ways to keep your cooler smelling fresh is to add a few drops of vanilla extract to a damp rag or paper towel, then wipe down the inside of the cooler before you put it away. The alcohol in the vanilla works as a disinfectant and your cooler will smell great!

Neutralize a Smelly Thermos

The easiest way to remove smells and stains from a thermos is by filling it with hot water and ½ cup baking soda, then letting it sit overnight. In the morning, just rinse well, and it should be good as new!

A Fresher Thermos

Put a teaspoon of salt inside your thermos before you store it to keep it fresh-smelling. For a larger cooler, try a charcoal briquette. It's surprising, but charcoal works as an air freshener.

Hair Dryer Trick

If you're having trouble cleaning off the baked-on grease and grime on your range's hood or other areas around your stove, make your job easier without the help of harsh commercial cleaners. Instead, warm it up by blasting it with your hair dryer. Once it's warm, it will wipe right off with a damp cloth.

Odor-Free Lunchbox

Kid's lunchbox starting to smell funky? Freshen it up with bread and vinegar! Just moisten a slice of bread with white vinegar and let it sit in the closed lunchbox overnight. In the morning, any bad odors should be gone.

Vanquish Smells with Vinegar

If you've burned dinner, welcome to the club. To get rid of the smoky scent (or any other strong kitchen odor), simply boil a cup of vinegar in 2 cups water. In 15 minutes, the smell should be gone. Or just dampen a cloth with a mixture of equal parts vinegar and water. Drape it over the cooking pot, taking care that the edges are far from the flame or intense heat.

Citrus to the Rescue

Smelly dishwasher? Just squeeze the juice of a lemon or orange into the liquid detergent compartment and run the dishwasher while it's empty, setting it to "steam dry." The citric acid will neutralize the odors caused by food-particle buildup. Now you can invite your guests into the kitchen without embarrassment!

Shiny Silver

In our house, shining silver was perpetually at the bottom of our to-do list and never made its way up until we realized you can shine silver with very little effort! After boiling potatoes, save the leftover water. Let tarnished silverware soak in the pot and simply rinse it clean after an hour.

Ring Toss

Get rid of the coffee ring in your mug by rubbing salt into it with an orange peel. The salt is abrasive and the citrus helps break up the stain.

The Best Way to Deodorize Your Freezer

Add a shallow bowl of freshly ground coffee, uncovered, to your freezer. Leave for a few days and any funky freezer odors will disappear.

Orange Oven

A self-cleaning oven can leave an odor after it's done its work. Eliminate the lingering smell by turning down the oven to 350° after the cleaning cycle, then placing a baking sheet lined with orange peels on the middle rack. Cook the peels for half an hour, and not only will the oven smell fresh, but your whole kitchen will too!

Make Your Home Smell Sugar-and-Spice Nice

For a great DIY home fragrance, simmer apple cider with a cinnamon stick and a few whole cloves. Also add a bit of orange peel, if you like. Your whole house will smell like your grandmother (real or imagined).

OUR FIVE FAVORITE
Ways to Freshen Up Your Garbage Disposal

1. A quick and easy way to deodorize your in-sink garbage disposal is to grind an orange or lemon peel inside it every so often. It will get rid of grease—and smell wonderful!

2. Cleaning your garbage disposal is as easy as throwing a few ice cubes down your drain. Run the disposal until you no longer hear grinding, and the job is done. The cold cubes will congeal any grease in the drain, allowing your disposal to break it up.

3. Instead of throwing away baking soda when it's finished its 30-day stint in your fridge, dump it down the garbage disposal with running water. It will keep your disposal fresh too!

4. Pour ½ cup salt down the drain of your kitchen sink with warm running water. This will freshen your drain and keep it from getting bogged down with grease.

5. Keep your garbage disposal running properly and odor-free with this simple once-a-month trick: Fill an ice-cube tray with white vinegar, and when frozen, grind about a dozen cubes. The ice sharpens the blades while the vinegar deodorizes the drain.

Dishwasher Done!

Soapy film coating your dishwasher? Run it on an empty cycle using vinegar instead of detergent. It will be sparkling clean, and your next load of dishes will be too.

Revitalize Plastic Containers

Washing a plastic container with a stale smell over and over won't get rid of the sour odor, but this will. Wipe inside with tomato juice, wash as usual, dry completely, and place in freezer (top and bottom separately). In a few days it will be good as new.

Keeping Trash Bins Clean

When cleaning your kitchen garbage can, sprinkle a little scouring powder at the bottom. This will soak up any liquids if your bag leaks and will also repel mildew and keep your bin smelling fresh.

OUR FIVE FAVORITE
Ways to Deodorize Your Fridge

1. When cleaning your refrigerator, don't use chemicals that can linger on your food and create nasty odors. After emptying the fridge, simply dissolve a cup of salt in a gallon of hot water and wipe away. Squeeze in the juice of a lemon for a nice scent.

2. It's an oldie, but a goodie! Simply open a box of baking soda and leave it in the back of your fridge. Shake the box a little each week and it will completely eliminate odors for a month or more.

3. Pour a little vanilla extract into a bottle cap and set in the refrigerator to absorb odors.

4. One of the best ways to eliminate odors from your refrigerator is to hollow out a grapefruit or orange, fill it with salt, and place in the back of the fridge. Leave it there until the salt gets completely damp, and then throw the whole thing out and replace.

5. We hate to throw anything away, so we love this way to repurpose used tea bags. Place them in a bowl and put them at the back of your refrigerator. They'll remove odors just as well as baking soda!

Airborne Toxic Event

Never cover your toothbrush between uses. Allowing the brush to air-dry is better than creating a closed, moist environment for bacteria to grow. You should also keep your toothbrush at least six feet away from your toilet, to keep it safely away from any bacteria that can become airborne when you flush.

Rub A Dub Dub

No matter how hard we scrub, we never seem to get the corners of our tub clean. Luckily, we have a clever solution! Soak cotton balls in your tub cleaner (or just some rubbing alcohol) and leave one in each corner of your tub overnight. By morning, they'll be as clear as day.

DIY Reed Diffuser

We love the look of a sophisticated reed diffuser in the bathroom, but hate the cost! Make your own and save some serious cash with this easy recipe. Find a small vase or container you like and buy a packet of diffuser reeds—often sold as "refills." First, pour a quarter-cup of mineral oil into a small bowl. Next add a couple of tablespoons of vodka and mix well. Then, add about 10 drops of your favorite essential oil and stir thoroughly. Finally, pour the mixture into the vase and put in five or six reeds. After a few hours, flip the reeds over and flip them again every few days. Enjoy your craftiness and extra dough!

DIY Scouring Powder

Make your own all-natural scouring powder by combining 1 cup salt with 1 cup baking soda. Store in a closed jar or can, and use it to scrub off hard water stains on your porcelain sinks and bathtub.

Cleaning Make-up Brushes

You should wash make-up brushes and sponges regularly to rid them of dirt, oil, and bacteria—none of which you want to transfer onto your face. Lather them up with baby shampoo, massage gently, and rinse in cool water. Let them air-dry.

Like-New Nail File

Ever wondered if there's a way to clean dirty emery boards? Just press transparent tape onto them, smooth over a bit, and peel off. Metal files can be cleaned with soap and water.

Great for Graters

What's the easiest way to clean a messy cheese grater? Reach for a lemon! Just rub the pulp-side of a cut lemon across a grater and it will clean off any stuck-on cheese.

Berry Clever

Those plastic baskets that berries come in are perfect for small items in your dishwasher. Just wedge in place and throw bottle tops, lids, and small utensils inside.

An Always-Fresh Bathroom

To create an automatic air freshener in the bathroom, we blot a bit of perfume or scented oil in the center of the toilet paper roll. Whenever someone uses it, the roll releases a pleasant whiff to keep the room smelling fresh.

Quick Sink Cleaner

Here's a quick and easy way to clean your bathroom sink: Just dampen a cotton rag or a bit of toilet paper with hydrogen peroxide and give it a few swipes! It's even great for sink stains, too.

Burning Hair Dryer Smell?

If it's beginning to smell like fire every time you blow-dry your hair, your dryer's motor may be clogged with hair and lint. Use an old toothbrush to brush clean the back of the dryer, where it sucks in air. Now you can do your hair without someone poking his head in the bathroom to make sure everything's OK!

DIY Daily Shower Spray

Stay on top of mold and mildew by keeping this daily shower spray within easy reach of all family members. Mix one part vinegar with 10 parts water in an empty spray bottle and you're ready to go. Bonus: You don't have to worry about a toxic cleaner hitting the baby's bath toys.

Mirror Makeover

For a unique cleaner for the mirrors around your home, use aerosol air freshener. It will bring your mirrors to a glossy shine and will have people wondering where that flowery scent is coming from.

Keep the Lid Up

This may go against years of training your boys, but in rarely used bathrooms the lid on the toilet should always be kept up. This allows air to circulate in the bowl, which will prevent mold and mildew from forming. Also, make sure to leave toilet lids up when you go on vacation!

—*Jennifer Pilcher, Olathe, KS*

CHAPTER 3

Keeping Your Clothes and Closets Fresh

All-Natural Fabric Softener

Here's an all-natural fabric softener that is also way less expensive than the store-bought kind. Just add ¼–½ cup baking soda to the wash cycle.

No More Dryer Sheets

Save on laundry products while you're saving the environment. Instead of buying fabric softener sheets, pick up a bottle of the liquid kind. Mix a solution of one-half fabric softener and one-half water, and put it into a spray bottle. For every laundry load, spritz onto a cloth and toss it in the dryer. A small amount (several sprays) will go a long way.

Less Expensive Laundry Gizmo

The secret, low-cost alternative to one of those balls that releases fabric softener during your laundry load? A clean kitchen sponge dampened with liquid fabric softener. Just put it in the washing machine once it's filled with water at the beginning of the load. It will slowly release the softener, just like the plastic balls do!

Stop Smells in Clothing

Do your clothes smell like mothballs or mildew? Simply washing them won't eradicate the smell, especially if it's caused by mothballs, which are oil-based. Instead, put five pieces of activated charcoal (charcoal that's been treated with oxygen, like the kind found in filters) into a paper bag and tape shut. Place the bag on top of a paper towel, and set it on top of your smelly clothes in a plastic bin or other closeable container. Cover the container and leave overnight—your clothes should smell as good as new in the morning!

Closet Scent Swap

Hate the smell of mothballs? Just use peppercorns instead! Buy the cheapest you can find, then pour into the toe of some old pantyhose, snip off the end, and knot. Then tie around a hook or hanger in your closet.

Cleaning Patent Leather

Patent leather shoes need a spruce-up? Believe it or not, the best cleaning solution is a glass cleaner like Windex. Spray onto a soft cloth and then use to buff patent leather shoes back to their old shine.

Bag Your Purses

If you're putting away a purse you don't think you'll use for a few weeks or a month, stuff some plastic grocery bags inside. This will ensure the purse keeps its shape— and give you something to do with those bags!

Lipstick on Your Collar?

To remove a lipstick stain from fabric, cover it with petroleum jelly for five minutes, then wash as usual. The glycerin in the jelly will break down the oils in the lipstick, making it easy to wash away.

Find the Stain

If you spilled something on a tablecloth or blanket, make the stain easy to find in the laundry room by clipping a bobby pin or safety pin onto the location. Find the pin and you've found the stain!

Save Scorched Fabric

Just because you scorched something with your iron doesn't mean it's a goner! Try this trick first: Lay a rag dampened in hydrogen peroxide (3 percent solution) over the scorch mark, then iron the rag with the iron set to medium heat. This isn't always safe for non-white fabrics, so try to test an inconspicuous spot first.

Erase Armpit Stains

Deodorant and antiperspirant stains often seem to sprout up out of nowhere, but you can tackle them with meat tenderizer! Aluminum compounds that bind to your clothes are what cause the yellow stain, but you can get rid of them with papain or bromelain, which are found in most meat tenderizers. Just add water to the tenderizer until it forms a paste, then rub on the stain and let sit for one hour before washing.

Toothbrush Trick

Have a mystery stain you can't get out? Try using the old toothbrush trick. First, apply some dishwashing liquid, or even just some laundry detergent, to the stain. Then rub in with an old toothbrush for about 30 seconds. The toothbrush will help penetrate the fibers of your clothes, even getting out worn-in stains.

Delicate Situation

You don't need to spend money on detergents just for delicates. Instead, use this homemade solution: 1 cup baking soda mixed with 1 cup warm water. The baking soda will clean your clothes without harming their delicate fibers.

Hamper Help

We feel bad throwing away used dryer sheets and now we don't have to. Instead, we place them at the bottom of the hamper to keep clothes fresh (a relative term) until we're ready to wash them.

Care for a Straw Hat

Keep your straw hat looking like new with hair spray. Spray evenly over the entire hat, then rub your hand gently over it to push in any fraying ends. The hair spray will keep them all in place, and your hat will look shinier than ever before!

Instant Lint Roller

If you have a Velcro hair roller you no longer use, repurpose it as a lint roller! It's perfect for rolling over sweaters and other clothes to pick up any stray pet hair or pills.

Diapers Love Vinegar

If you use cloth diapers, soak them before you wash them in a mixture of 1 cup white vinegar for every 9 quarts water. It will balance out the pH, neutralizing urine and keeping the diapers from staining. Vinegar is also said to help prevent diaper rash.

Baking Soda for Baby Mamas

Baking soda is a gift to anyone who is feeding an infant. Keep some on hand, and if (and when) your baby spits up, sprinkle baking soda on the spot to neutralize odors and absorb the spill before it sets.

Steam Away Smoke

To remove a smoky smell from your clothes, fill your bathtub with hot water and add 1 cup white vinegar. Then just hang the clothes above the steaming water, and the smoke smell will dissipate in about a half hour. Ah, vinegar—is there anything it can't do?

Tobacco Killer

Get stubborn odors left behind by cigarettes off clothes by adding a half a cup of baking soda to the wash cycle when doing your laundry.

Fight with Fizz

If your clothes are extra greasy, add a can of lemon-lime soda to your washing machine along with detergent. The acid in the soda breaks down the oil in the greasy clothes, and your wash will sparkle.

Solving a Gasoline Problem

Nothing stinks on your clothes like gasoline! To remove the odor, place the offending clothes in a bucket of cold water, and add a can of cola and a cup of baking soda. Soak overnight, then line dry outside if possible. If there is still any odor left, just wash as usual and it should be gone.

Storing Leather and Suede

When storing leather and suede garments, don't cover them in plastic. These materials need a little breathing space, or they'll quickly dry out.

A Coat of Coffee Does the Trick

If your black cotton items are starting to look more like they're dark blue, wash a load of only black items. But first, brew a strong pot of black coffee, then add it to the rinse cycle.

Give Your Leather a Pick-Me-Up

To revive the beauty of leather, lightly beat two egg whites and then apply to the leather with a soft sponge. Allow the egg whites to remain on the leather for 3–5 minutes, and then wipe off with a soft cloth dampened with warm water. Dry immediately and buff off any residue.

How to Scrub Away Scuffs

If you have black scuff marks on shoes, luggage, or other items, try rubbing lemon juice on them. Rubbing alcohol also works well.

OUR FIVE FAVORITE
Ways to Freshen Shoes

1. Get rid of nasty shoe odors by sprinkling salt in them and leaving overnight. The salt will absorb moisture and odors.

2. Place a fabric softener sheet in your shoes overnight to get rid of any foul odors. This also works for hampers, gym bags, or anything else that needs a little freshening.

3. Here's another great tip for preventing smelly shoes. Take a couple of old socks without holes and fill them with scented cat litter. Then place them in the shoes when you're not wearing them. They'll suck up any moisture—and odor.

4. To keep your shoes smelling better, store them in the freezer! It sounds funny, but it's true: The cold temperature slows down the growth of microscopic funkiness-makers.

5. Break up a few leaves of sage and spread them around inside your shoes. They'll kill the bacteria that causes foot odor. To cut down on how much you perspire in the first place, try drinking sage tea. Herbalists say it will take several weeks, but you'll see results!

Candles for Your Closet

We love this cheap, environmentally friendly air freshener for your closet. All you need is an old, burned-up candle with a strong scent. Chop the leftover wax into chunks, slip it into an unused (but clean!) sock, and tie the sock closed. Tie it around a hanger or hang from a hook. It will freshen your closet with the scent of the candle!

Lift Up Mud Stains

Have the kids come home with fresh mud stains on their clothes? Don't apply water! Instead, let the mud dry, then use a piece of packing or duct tape to lift up all of the hardened dirt you can. Then wash as usual.

Smell the Roses Every Day

Clean laundry loses its fresh scent quickly when sitting in stuffy drawers and closets. To keep your clothes, lingerie, and linens smelling freshly washed all the time, place fabric softener sheets in your dresser drawers.

CHAPTER 4

DIY Air Fresheners and Potpourri

Refresh Potpourri

If your favorite potpourri loses its scent, it's easy to revive—with vodka. Yep, you read that right. Just pour a little vodka into a spray bottle and spritz the potpourri, mixing it up so each piece is saturated.

"Orange" You Glad?

Make a great homemade air freshener with an orange: Just cut it in half, remove the pulp, and fill with salt. It's easy, effective, and cheap!

Make a Room Smell Wonderful

Who hasn't wanted to make a beautiful bouquet of flowers last longer? Give your flower petals a second life by layering them with non-iodized salt in a small jar. This works best with flowers that have pulpy petals and woody stems, like roses, lavender, and honeysuckle. The salt will bring out their natural scent and help freshen your entire room. Keep a lid on the jar when you're not around to make the scent last even longer.

Spicy Scent

Bring seasonal scents into your home during the holidays without buying manufactured home fragrances—customize your own spice potpourri instead! Select a few favorite spices from your kitchen and place them in an old nylon stocking; tie the ends closed. Store the sachet near a cracked-open window, fan, or heating vent, and savor the spices of the season.

Super-Power Your Potpourri

Hide a charcoal briquette in your potpourri bowl and it will absorb foul odors. Charcoal absorbs moisture, which will also help stop mold and mildew buildup in the bathroom. Make sure to use briquettes that haven't been soaked in lighter fluid and enjoy your newly odor-free bathroom!

DIY Air Freshener Refills

Do you have a plug-in air freshener? You may be able to refill it without buying costly refills that contain toxic chemicals. Instead, use essential oil, which comes in a variety of scents and can be found online or in health-food stores. Remove the wick from the bulb, fill with half water and half essential oil, give it a shake, and put the wick back in. Then plug in for a pleasing scent!

DIY Freshness

Make your own gel air fresheners at home with this simple recipe: Boil a cup of water, then mix in 1 packet gelatin, 1 tablespoon salt, 15 drops of your favorite essential oil, and several drops of food coloring. Once the gelatin dissolves, pour into a glass cup or jar to set. Keep away from kids and pets and enjoy the scent for a month or more!

Potpourri Substitute

Instead of spending money on costly potpourri, use this inexpensive trick to give your house a delightful aroma. Heat your oven to 250°, toss some ground cinnamon on a sheet of foil, and leave the door slightly ajar. The cinnamon will unleash its delicious aroma for about 15–20 minutes, giving your home a delightful scent.

—*Evelyn Quigley*

OUR FIVE FAVORITE
Ways to Neutralize Odors Before They Begin

1. Vinegar is so perfect for neutralizing odors and cutting back on dust, we like to keep a little in a small jar near heating vents. Our favorite Who Knew? hero will leave your room smelling cleaner than it ever did with an air freshener. Just make sure to replace it once a week.

2. Make a dehumidifier for your basement or other musty areas at no cost. Fill a coffee can with charcoal briquettes and punch a few holes in the lid. Place it in damp areas, and replace the charcoal once a month as it absorbs the humidity.

3. Baking soda is not just for the fridge. Place some in a bowl or decorative jar near the changing table, in the bathroom, or near the litter box and it will help keep your home smelling fresher.

4. Purify the air without an air filter by buying potted plants that naturally clean your air. Some good choices are rubber trees, corn plants, bamboo palm, ficus, mums, gerbera daisies, English ivy, peace lily, and philodendrons.

5. If your kids have outgrown sidewalk chalk or you happen to have some around, place it in the damp areas of your home (like your basement) to absorb excess moisture and repel mildew. Use a container that allows air to get through it, like a mesh bag, coffee can, or paper bag with holes poked in it.

Revitalize Dusty Potpourri

If your potpourri is looking dusty, here's an easy trick to clean it: Pour the potpourri into a plastic zip-tight bag, seal the top, and use a fork to poke some small holes into the bag. Shake the bag over a garbage can to catch all the dirt and dust that will fall through the holes. Now your potpourri will be as good as new!

Long-Lasting Air Freshener

Are you disappointed when an air-freshening spray's scent only lasts a few minutes? Put some Styrofoam packing peanuts into a jar and spray them with the air freshener. The foam will lock in the pleasant scent, making it last for days or even weeks!

Very Vanilla

If you love the aroma of vanilla, make an air freshener using vanilla's enticing scent. Just take a small jar and place several cotton balls inside. Squeeze a few drops of vanilla extract onto the cotton balls. Before putting the cover on the jar, use a nail to puncture a few holes into it and *voilà*! You've got your very own vanilla air freshener!

Make Your Own Country Air Freshener

Save tons of money on air fresheners with this easy DIY one! Put a half cup of baking soda in a jar and then take your favorite essential oil and put about 10 drops into the baking soda. Mix well. Next, find a cute piece of fabric from your scraps collection and cut it into a circle slightly larger than the top of the jar. Finally, place the fabric on top of the jar and tie a ribbon around the fabric and jar to secure it. Now you have an adorable air freshener that brightens any room!

Lemon Fresh Spray

Avoid all the chemicals in store-bought air-freshener sprays with this homemade version made with lemon juice. Lemons are natural deodorizers and will give your home a pleasing scent, while keeping the air safe for children, pets, and plants. Combine 1 teaspoon baking soda with 2 teaspoons lemon juice in a spray bottle. Add 2 cups of hot water and shake the mixture until the baking soda dissolves. Let cool. Spray as needed when things get stinky!

CHAPTER 5

A Fresh Home for Your Pets

Shampoo-dle

If your dog hates taking baths, try placing a towel at the bottom of the tub before you fill it up. It will be much less slippery under your dog's paws, and that will help keep him calm.

Puppy Pet-icure

The best time to clip your dog's nails is after he's had a bath or has been swimming. The water will soften the hard outer coating of your pet's nails, making them easier to cut.

Remove Gooey Gum

If your dog has ever stepped in gum while you were out for a walk, you know how hard it can be to remove the sticky substance from between his pads. Thankfully, you can make it a little easier with some olive or vegetable oil. Rub oil all over the gum, then pull it out with your fingers or a comb. The oil will help lubricate the gum and remove it more easily. And it will even moisturize your pet's pads!

Housebreaking Help

Housebreaking your new puppy is the hardest part about being a new dog parent, but you can make it a little easier with this tip. If your puppy has soiled newspaper, bury it just underneath the soil where you'd like him to relieve himself outside. The smell will tell him it's the right place to go.

Eradicate Pet Odors Permanently

If your pet had an accident on your rug he'll probably keep going back to the spot if you don't eliminate the odor completely. After blotting the stain, pour some cornmeal on it and let it sit for 2 hours before vacuuming up the grains. The cornmeal will absorb any lingering odors, breaking the cycle of indoor pet accidents.

Eliminating Cat Smell

If the smell from your in-heat housecat's spray has more than nine lives, try mixing 1 cup hydrogen peroxide with ½ tablespoon baking soda and 2 squirts liquid dish soap. Pour into a spray bottle and use wherever Fluffy has left her trademark. (Be sure to spot-check, as you run the risk of bleaching certain materials.)

Expel Urine Smell

If your pet had an accident on your couch and you just can't get rid of the smell, try this solution. In an empty spray bottle, combine 2 parts water to 1 part mouthwash. Spray the mixture onto the soiled upholstery. Next, lay newspaper over the sprayed area and let dry. The newspaper should absorb the smell completely. If not, repeat the process. Your cushions may smell minty-fresh for a few days, but once that wears off the urine smell will be gone!

Conquer Cat Allergies

It's not just fur that causes allergies, but dander, saliva, and urine particles. If you keep your cat's litter box inside, clean it out before allergic friends come over and they'll have a better time.

No More Fuzzy View

If you have a cat who loves looking out the window, you know how full of cat hair the screen can get when he presses himself against it for a closer look outside. An easy fix? Just run a lint roller across the screen, or press a piece of tape against it.

Kitty Litter Cure

Here's a fantastic use for used tea bags. Let them dry, then cut them open. Mix the used tea with your kitty litter to keep it smelling extra fresh.

OUR FIVE FAVORITE
Easy Ways to Remove Pet Hair

1. If you don't have the heart to banish your pet from the couch, here's a solution for removing all that hair from your sofa. Just use a dry, unused dish sponge to wipe the hair into a pile with your hand. Discard the hair and then repeat the process. After you've gotten most of the hair, take a sheet of fabric softener from the laundry room and use it to pick up the rest—the hair will be naturally attracted to it. When that's done, use a vacuum cleaner to add the finishing touch.

2. Uh oh, guests are on their way and you've just noticed a cat-fur nest all over your couch. To quickly remove pet hair from furniture, turn to your rubber dishwashing gloves, then rub the offending furniture with them. The hair will stick to the gloves and you can quickly throw it away.

3. To get pet hair off of any surface, just blow up a balloon and rub it across the material. The hair will be attracted to the static electricity of the balloon and become attached to it instead of your pants or chair.

4. Sometimes the simplest ideas are the best: Just take a piece of packing tape, sticky side up, to the hair-covered material and remove the hair easily.

5. Stop the problem before it starts by vacuuming your dog (yes, really!). Use your vacuum cleaner's brush attachment and stroke your dog gently. It won't hurt him and he may even come to enjoy it.

CHAPTER 6

Eliminating Smells in Your Car and Outdoors

Got a Stink in Your Car?

Instead of buying a commercial freshener, repurpose a sheet of fabric softener to help sweeten the air. Place sheets under the car seats, in door pockets, or in the trunk to keep your car smelling fresh.

Freshen Your Car

There's an even better use for your car's ashtrays than spent cigarette butts. Fill them with baking soda and they'll keep your car odor-free. You won't have to resort

to those annoying pine tree–shaped air fresheners.
Replace the baking soda every two or three months.

Free Floor Mats

Floor mats getting funky? If your car's floor mats need to
be replaced, consider going to a carpet store and finding some samples to use instead. You'll always be able
to find samples that are gray or another color to match
your car's interior, and best of all, they're free!

Cloves in the Car

Do you hate the smell of store-bought car air fresheners?
An easy and great-smelling substitute is to simply take a
handful of cloves and put them in your car's ashtrays or
cup holders. The sweet scent will freshen up your car in
no time—for pennies!

Bumper Sticker Remover

If it's finally time to remove that bumper sticker from the 2004
election, use hand sanitizer to make the job easier. Rub it
into the sticker and let sit for 15 minutes. It will help dissolve the glue and will practically wipe right off!

Stop Smoky Smells

Did you know that a bowl of sliced apples will remove the smell of cigarette smoke in an enclosed space? If there's a smoky smell in your car, place some cut-up apples in it overnight and it will be gone by morning.

Cute Car Freshener

Here's a way to personalize your car and make it smell delicious. Find an image you like online, make two printouts, and cut them out. Next, glue each printout to a cereal box and cut out around each shape again, so you have two cardboard-backed images. Now take a new dish sponge and cut it out in the same shape. Glue one image to each side of the sponge with superglue. Next, use a needle to thread a string through the top of the sponge and tie it in a loop. Finally, squeeze about 10 drops of your favorite essential oil onto the sponge and hang in the car. The best part is you can just add a few more drops of essential oil when the scent starts to fade!

OUR FAVORITE
Ways to Clean Outdoor Furniture

1. Get wicker furniture front-porch ready for summer. Blow-dry off the loose dirt, then clean with white vinegar and warm salt water, and apply a coat of lemon oil.

2. If you have mold on your plastic resin outdoor furniture, get it summer-ready by mixing a paste of lemon and salt. Polish it on in a circular motion, rinse, and leave to sun-dry.

3. Here's a quick and easy way to clean plastic outdoor furniture: Use shaving cream! Apply a layer with a damp rag or sponge to your furniture, let sit for 10 minutes, then spray down with the hose. (For super-dirty furniture, rinse before and after applying the shaving cream.) It will look almost as good as new!

4. To clean outdoor seat cushions, make a solution of 1 teaspoon dishwashing detergent, 1 quart warm water, and 1 tablespoon borax in a spray bottle and shake well. Spray directly onto both sides of cushions, completely saturating them. Let them stand for 15 minutes and then wash off the solution by spraying the cushions with the hose. Stand them on their edges and let them dry out of direct sunlight.

5. The laziest way to clean plastic or resin patio furniture? Just toss it in the swimming pool before going to bed, and in the morning it'll be good as new. Meanwhile, your pool's filter will clean up the dirt.

Silence Squeaky Lawn Furniture

If your wicker seems to scream every time you sit in it, it's become too dry. Take off any cushions and spray the wicker with a hose. The water will give it enough moisture to silence the squeaks.

No More Kiddie Pool Clean-Up

Don't let leaves and grime get into your kiddie pool when your little ones aren't using it—it's easy to make your own cover. With a pair of scissors, cut a small *x* into each corner of an old plastic shower curtain. Then cut two wire hangers into two *v* shapes, and use them as stakes by threading them through each *x*.

Doormats

Your porch's doormat can be cleaned with a sprinkling of baking soda. Brush vigorously and then sweep away the dirt. The next time it rains, the job will be complete.

OUR FIVE FAVORITE
Ways to Get Rid of Sidewalk and Driveway Stains

1. Got stains on paving stones or a concrete patio? Try pouring hot water from several feet above the stone onto the stain. Repeat several times, and your stain may just disappear. If this doesn't work, try rubbing some dishwashing liquid into the spot with a toothbrush, then rinsing off. For really tough stains, add a bit of ammonia to the water.

2. Unsightly marks on sidewalks and patios are often caused by tar, gum, and pet urine. These can usually be removed with vinegar, so if you're having trouble removing a stain from concrete, try dousing it with vinegar and letting it sit for a day.

3. If you have rust stains on your concrete, pour on a little cola and let it sit. By the next time it rains, the stains will be gone. —*Jess Holman, Syracuse, NY*

4. Cleaning oil spots off the driveway is difficult, and the cleaners can be quite expensive. Instead, sprinkle baking soda over the stains, then rub with a wet scrub brush soaked with hot water. The baking soda breaks apart oil particles, so with a little elbow grease, you can have your driveway looking new in no time.

5. Want to get rid of the grass growing in the cracks of your sidewalk or patio? Make a mixture of salt and baking soda and sprinkle it into the cracks.

BONUS CHAPTER!

A Bug-Free Home

Beat Back Bugs with Vicks

Spending some time outdoors at a picnic or barbecue? Rub some Vicks VapoRub on your wrists and ankles to repel insects. They hate the smell and will leave you alone!

No More Gnats

Tiny little gnats are probably some of the most annoying bugs out there. When you see their telltale clouds, rub some baby oil on yourself to keep them away from you.

Fight Flies

Are giant horseflies driving you crazy? Next time you go outside, rub mouthwash on your body and enjoy the serenity of a fly-free experience.

Adios Ants!

Planning a barbecue and want to make sure the ants don't come marching by? Take a piece of charcoal, crumble it up, and spread the pieces around the perimeter of your picnic area. The ants will avoid the area, leaving you to enjoy the food!

Kill Ants Dead

If you have an ant infestation in your home, here's an inexpensive way to kill them, without calling the exterminator. Mix a quarter cup sugar, 1 teaspoon borax, and 1 cup water in a small container (not one that you eat out of) and pour a bit of the mixture into some bottle caps. Place the caps wherever you see ants. They will carry the poison back to the colony, killing the whole nest. Borax can be found at drugstores. Be careful, this mixture is not safe for pets or kids to ingest.

Stop an Ant Infestation

If it seems like ants are taking over your house, try this easy remedy: Sprinkle talcum powder along your baseboards and doorways. It dehydrates their bodies, eventually killing them.

Save Your Houseplants

Have you noticed tiny, fragile webs in your houseplants? You probably have spider mites living there. To get rid of them, gently wipe some buttermilk on the leaves and stems. They should disappear, leaving your plants healthy and green again.

No More Aphids

Aphids eating up your plants? Pour ¼ teaspoon eucalyptus oil, ½ teaspoon dishwashing liquid, ½ teaspoon corn oil, and 2 quarts water in a spray bottle and shake well to combine. Spray the mixture on your plants to kill aphids fast.

Plant Rescue

Save your plants from aphids with this simple formula:
Boil 1 pint of water and add 1 lemon's worth of zest.
Let steep overnight. In the morning, strain the rind if
desired. Pour liquid into a spray bottle and spray it on
your plants. Soon, aphids will be a thing of the past.

Bye-Bye Buggy Plants

Keep bugs away from your houseplants with garlic.
Place a peeled garlic clove, narrow end up, just under
the soil of your houseplant. Creepy-crawlers will stay
away from your plants!

Use for Potato Water

Making sweet potatoes for dinner? Save the water you
boil them in and put it into a spray bottle. Spray the
liquid wherever you see ants or aphids on your houseplants, and they'll soon be gone.

Orange Peel Answer

You may find the smell of oranges delicious, but flies
don't! The next time you eat an orange, save the rind and
leave it out on your countertop. It will keep flies away.

Barbecue Bugs Be Gone!

Do mosquitoes hover over the grill when you barbecue? Next time, place a few sprigs of rosemary or sage on top of the coals. They'll repel mosquitoes, leaving your meat in peace.

Spicy Solution

If your backyard is overrun with bugs, try this spicy solution to keep them away. Dice up 2–3 habanero peppers, 2 large onions, and 3 garlic cloves. Add peppers, onions, and garlic cloves to 1 quart of boiling water. Let steep for several hours, then strain into a spray bottle. Before spending some time outside, spray the mixture all over your yard to get rid of all bugs.

Houseplant Insect Spray

Say goodbye to insects in your houseplants with this formula, which is especially great for meal bugs. Just pour 2–3 tablespoons of dry laundry soap and 1 quart of warm water into a spray container and shake well. Spray the solution onto plants immediately; this solution cannot be stored and must be made fresh for each use.

OUR TOP FIVE
Ways To Get Rid of Ants

1. Use caulk to seal any cracks you see in your walls, doorways, and windows. Aside from keeping out creepy-crawlers, this will also lower your energy bill!

2. Ants don't like the scent of vinegar, peppermint oil, cinnamon, black pepper, cayenne pepper, whole cloves, and bay leaves. Spread some of these items around your baseboards and doorways to repel the ants.

3. If you see a line of ants, get out your vacuum cleaner and suck them up! Then vacuum up some talcum powder, which will dehydrate them, so they don't make a new home in your appliance.

4. If your yard or garden is infested with pesky ants, sprinkle artificial sweetener (anything with aspartame) over the affected areas. Or try oats, cornmeal, instant grits, or cream of wheat. The ants will eat the dry cereal, which will then absorb all the moisture in their bodies and kill them.

5. If you know where the nest is, pour several gallons of boiling water into it. This should kill them all, leaving your house ant-free!

Say "*Sayonara*" to Spiders

Do you have a spider problem in your home? Just put some cedar chips into a few pairs of old pantyhose and hang them around your house. The spiders will be gone in no time.

Eradicate Raccoons

Raccoons keep getting into your trash, and so far your only strategy is running outside to yell at them every night. Save your screaming and purchase some inexpensive Epsom salts from a drugstore. Sprinkle them on and around your garbage cans and raccoons will stay away, but your pets will be safe!

Goodbye, Mealworms

Never worry about mealworms getting into your pasta, rice, or flour again! Just spread bay leaves around your cabinets. Mealworms hate the smell, and will stay away.

Mosquito Magic

Mosquitoes are a pain each summer, but you don't have to buy citronella candles, mosquito coils, or the latest gadget—you can just use cardboard egg cartons and coffee trays (the kind you get when you order more than a couple of coffees to-go). Light them on fire, then blow them out and let them smolder in a fire-safe location. The burning smell they produce is pleasant, but keeps mosquitoes away.

—*Chantal Landry*

Befuddle Birds

Birds (and their droppings) driving you crazy on your deck? Keep them away with baking or baby powder. Sprinkle it where they like to land, and they'll find somewhere else to go. They hate the feeling of it under their feet!

Rodent Remover

It won't surprise you if you've ever smelled them, but mothballs repel rodents, too. To use them to get rid of mice or rats around your home, place five of them in a Ziploc bag and smash until they're a powder. Then put in a spray bottle along with a squirt of dishwashing liquid and fill with water. Spray around baseboards and any-where you see pests, but keep away from kids and pets.

Stop Wasps

Is there anything worse than coming upon a swarm of wasps when you're enjoying your garden? If you find that wasps are building a nest in the same spot year after year, spray the area with white vinegar several times in the beginning of the spring and they'll find somewhere else to roost.

Avoid an Ant Infestation

Never use decorative paving stones near your home. Certain ants love to make their homes underneath them! Use them away from your house to be certain ants won't decide to come in for a visit.

Ant Antics

Draw a line ants won't cross—with chalk! Ants think chalk is ash and won't cross it (because it may be a sign of fire). Use their tiny brains against them by drawing a thick line of chalk along windowsills, cabinets, or anywhere else they enter your home. You can even draw a line on your picnic table!

Tennis, Anyone?

If aphids are infesting your plants, here's an easy solution. Cover a tennis ball with petroleum jelly and leave it nearby. The bugs will be attracted to its bright color, and then get stuck on its side.

Fruit Fly Fix

Have a fruit fly problem? Add a couple of drops of dish-washing liquid to a bowl of apple cider vinegar and leave it where you see flies. The smell of the vinegar attracts the flies, while the dish soap breaks the surface tension of the vinegar and causes the little nuisances to drown.

Repels Vampires, Too

Citronella candles are great for repelling insects, but they can be pricey. Get the same effect for much cheaper by mixing garlic with water and spraying it near all your outdoor light bulbs. As the bulbs heat up, they spread a faint garlicky scent across your yard, which will keep mosquitoes and other bugs away.

Bunny Buster

Are rabbits overrunning your garden? Keep them away with the help of some vinegar. First poke a few holes in a pill bottle, then soak 3–4 cotton balls with vinegar and place them inside. Bury them just under the soil and the smell will keep rabbits away.

No More Squirrels in the Bird Feeder

This idea may conjure up a cartoon chase scene, but here's a safe, natural way to feed the birds and not the squirrels: Simply rub shortening on the pole leading up to your feeder to keep the uninvited guests from letting themselves in.

Bug-Free Plants

Add pencil shavings to your houseplants if they suffer from bug infestation. Bugs don't like the smell of the cedar in pencils. Just mix in with the soil, mostly at the bottom.

An Answer to Ants

Flour mixed with cayenne pepper makes a great barrier to ants in your cabinets. You can also sprinkle outside wherever ants are infesting your garden or yard. Ants will run for shelter and you can sweep up the powder. Try ½ tablespoon pepper together with ½ cup white flour (sifted makes it easier).

So Long, Slugs

If slugs are finding their way into your container plants, cover the hole with used sanding disks or cut a circle of sandpaper big enough to cover the hole. Simply place underneath the pot, making sure to it line up so the hole is fully covered. Slugs hate the scratchy surface and won't cross it.

Roach Killer

Chasing, banging with a shoe, squishing—none of them are failsafe and they're all gross when it comes to getting rid of roaches. Go for the kill by zapping them with WD-40 instead of bug spray.

Evict Silverfish with Spices

Silverfish like to hang around damp places, but they'll slither away if you decorate with spice sachets. Try combining sage, bay leaves, and apple pie spices in fabric bags and hanging in the kitchen, bathroom, basement, and other moist areas. You can also scatter whole cloves around.

Index

who knew?™
online

VISIT OUR WEBSITE AT WhoKnewTips.com!

- Money-saving tips
- Quick 'n' easy recipes
- Who Knew? books and ebooks
- And much more!

Facebook.com/WhoKnewTips
Daily tips, giveaways, and more fun!

Twitter.com/WhoKnewTips
Get a free daily tip and ask us your questions

YouTube.com/WhoKnewTips
Watch demos of your favorite tips

Pinterest.com/WhoKnewTips
Hot tips from around the web!